The Little Book
of Neuroscience
Haikus

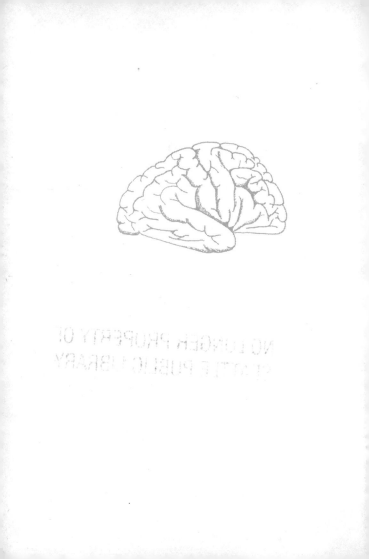

The Little Book of Neuroscience Haikus

ERIC H. CHUDLER

ILLUSTRATIONS BY DIANA ELISABETH DUBE

W. W. NORTON & COMPANY

NEW YORK · LONDON

Previous edition published as ELEPHANT ON BRAIN:
The Nervous System in 17 Syllables

For information about permission to reproduce selections from
this book, write to Permissions, W. W. Norton & Company, Inc.,
500 Fifth Avenue, New York, NY 10110

For information about special discounts for bulk purchases,
please contact W. W. Norton Special Sales at
specialsales@wwnorton.com or 800-233-4830

Manufacturing by Edward Brothers Malloy
Book design by Molly Heron
Production manager: Leeann Graham

Library of Congress Cataloging-in-Publication Data

Chudler, Eric H.
[Elephant on brain]
The little book of neuroscience haikus / Eric H. Chudler ;
illustrations by Diana Elisabeth Dube.
pages cm
Originally published: Elephant on brain,
published approximately 2010.
ISBN 978-0-393-70832-5 (pbk.)
1. Neurosciences—Miscellanea. 2. Neurosciences—Poetry.
3. Brain—Miscellanea. I. Title.
RC341.C538 2013
616.8—dc23

2013003146

ISBN: 978-0-393-70832-5 (pbk.)

W. W. Norton & Company, Inc.
500 Fifth Avenue, New York, N.Y. 10110
www.wwnorton.com

W. W. Norton & Company Ltd.
Castle House, 75/76 Wells Street, London W1T 3QT

1 2 3 4 5 6 7 8 9 0

CONTENTS

INTRODUCTION

WHY WRITE POEMS ABOUT THE BRAIN?

The brain has fascinated philosophers and scientists for centuries. Poetry allows writers to express thoughts in creative and novel ways, and I enjoy the challenge of writing short poems about the brain. Each word must be chosen carefully to provide readers with the essence of the poem.

WHAT POETRY STYLE IS USED IN THIS BOOK?

The poems are similar to Japanese haiku. Each poem is three lines containing five syllables, seven syllables, and five syllables.

YOU CALL THIS POETRY? ANYONE COULD DO THIS!
I am glad you think so and hope you will write
your own poems.

The Little Book
of Neuroscience
Haikus

PLACES

Axon to synapse
Electrical, chemical
Signals for the brain.

NEURONS (nerve cells) have specialized extensions called dendrites and axons. Dendrites bring information to the cell body and axons take information away from the cell body. Inside a neuron, electrical signals send information down the axon. Information flows from one neuron to another neuron at the synapse using chemicals called neurotransmitters.

Neuronal membrane
Membrane-bound vesicles fuse
Spill contents in gap.

VESICLES are membrane-bound sacs that contain neurotransmitters. At the synapse, an electrical impulse triggers the migration of vesicles. The membrane of the vesicles fuses with the membrane of the terminal. This action releases neurotransmitters into the synaptic gap.

Who, what, when, where, why
Electrochemical signs
Three pounds of tissue.

NEURONS send messages through an exchange of electrically charged chemicals. These messages are responsible for all functions of the 3-pound human brain.

Hot, cold, hot, cold, warm
Thermostat regulating
Hypothalamus.

THE HYPOTHALAMUS is located at the base of the brain. Although the hypothalamus is only the size of a pea (about 1/300 of the total brain weight), it is responsible for important functions such as the control of body temperature. The hypothalamus acts like a thermostat by sensing changes in body temperature and then sending signals to different parts of the body to adjust the temperature. For example, if you are too hot, the hypothalamus detects this and then sends a signal to expand the capillaries in your skin. This causes blood to be cooled faster and body temperature to drop.

Cerebral cortex
Surrounding outer layer
I think about thoughts.

THE CEREBRAL CORTEX is the outermost layer of the brain. In fact, the word *cortex* comes from the Latin word meaning "bark of a tree." This area of the brain is responsible for higher-order cognitive processes such as language, decision making, reasoning, and complex thought.

Integrates signals
Traffic control, thalamus
Sensory, motor.

THE THALAMUS receives sensory information and relays this information to the cerebral cortex. The cerebral cortex also sends information to the thalamus, which then transmits this information to other areas of the brain and spinal cord to control movement.

Gyri, sulci show
Undulating bumps, valleys
Brain's convolutions.

WHEN THE BRAIN is removed from the skull, it looks a bit like a large pinkish walnut with many bumps and grooves. The sulci (or fissures) are the grooves and the gyri are the bumps on the outside surface of the brain. The folding produced by these bumps and grooves increases the amount of cerebral cortex that can fit inside the skull. In fact, the total surface area of the cerebral cortex is approximately 324 square inches—about the size of a full page of newspaper. Although most people have the same patterns of gyri and sulci on the cerebral cortex, no two brains are exactly alike.

Maintaining balance
Cerebellum, little brain
Aids motor learning.

THE WORD *cerebellum* comes from the Latin word for "little brain." The cerebellum is located behind the brain stem and is similar to the cerebral cortex in that it is divided into hemispheres and has a cortex that surrounds these hemispheres. The cerebellum is important for maintaining posture, coordinating movement, and motor learning.

Spinal cord highway
Central, peripheral tied
Signals back and forth.

THE SPINAL CORD is the pathway that connects the central and peripheral nervous systems. The spinal cord is about 45 centimeters long in men and 43 centimeters long in women. It is composed of 31 segments: 8 cervical, 12 thoracic, 5 lumbar, 5 sacral, and 1 coccygeal; a pair of spinal nerves exits from each segment. The length of the spinal cord is much shorter than the length of the bony spinal column. In fact, the spinal cord extends down only to the last of the thoracic vertebrae. Therefore, nerves that branch from the spinal cord from the lumbar and sacral levels must run in the vertebral canal for a distance before they exit the vertebral column.

Stem of brain tissue
Most basic of life functions
Automatically.

THE BRAIN STEM is a general term for the area of the
brain between the thalamus and spinal cord. Structures within the brain stem include the medulla,
pons, tectum, reticular formation, and tegmentum.
Some of these areas are responsible for the most
basic functions of life such as breathing, heart rate,
and blood pressure.

Fight-or-flight response
Activate sympathetic
Escape angry bear.

THE ORGANS (the "viscera") of our body, such as
the heart, stomach, and intestines, are regulated by
a part of the nervous system called the autonomic
nervous system. The autonomic nervous system is
divided into the sympathetic and parasympathetic
nervous systems. These systems are part of the
peripheral nervous system and control many organs
and muscles within the body. In most situations, we
are unaware of the workings of the autonomic nervous system because it functions in an involuntary,
reflexive manner. In emergencies that cause stress
and require us to fight or take flight, the sympathetic
nervous system is activated, causing blood pressure
to rise and the heart to beat faster.

A warm, sunny day
Parasympathetic time
Let's rest and digest.

THE PARASYMPATHETIC nervous system is the other part of the autonomic nervous system. In times when there is no emergency, the parasympathetic nervous system works to save energy when blood pressure decreases, heartbeat slows, and digestion can start. This is the time to "rest and digest."

They call it vagus
Both sensory and motor
Wandering tenth nerve.

THE VAGUS nerve is the tenth cranial nerve. The word *vagus* comes from the Latin word meaning "wandering." This long nerve travels to various organs and glands to control sensory, motor, and autonomic functions such as digestion and heart rate.

One hundred billion
Cells within the cranium
Amazing neurons.

THE HUMAN BRAIN contains an estimated 100 billion
neurons (nerve cells).

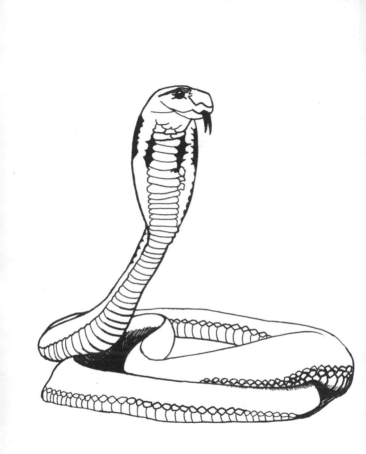

Spiders, snakes, oh my
Almond-shaped amygdala
Interpreting fear.

THE AMYGDALA is an almond-shaped, limbic structure located in the temporal lobe of the brain. The
amygdala is important for memory of emotional
responses, including fear.

Massive frontal lobe
Planning, emotions, movement
Problem solving too.

THE FRONTAL LOBE is responsible for many higher cognitive functions. By volume, the frontal lobe is the largest (41%) of the four lobes of the cerebral cortex.

Touch, pain, temperature
Somatosensory sense
Parietal lobe.

THE PARIETAL LOBE of the cerebral cortex is involved with the perception of the somatosensory senses, including touch, pressure, pain, and temperature.

Cortical columns
Functionally organized
Occipital lobe

THE OCCIPITAL LOBE is responsible for the perception of visual information. Neurons in the occipital lobe are organized in columns, where each neuron in a column has similar receptive fields.

Temporal lobe role
Hearing, memory, language
I can hear you now.

THE TEMPORAL LOBE is important for hearing, memory, and language.

Blood-brain barrier
Microwaves, radiation
Open sesame.

THE BLOOD-BRAIN barrier, created by tight-fitting endothelial cells that surround blood vessels, limits materials in the blood from entering the brain. The blood-brain barrier can be broken down by microwaves and radiation, permitting the entry of chemicals into the brain's blood supply.

THINGS

Memory fleeting
Cannot remember who, what
No hippocampus.

THE HIPPOCAMPUS is a brain structure involved in the complex processes of forming, sorting, and storing memories. Damage to the hippocampus can cause anterograde amnesia, a condition in which people can remember the distant past and learn new skills, but they cannot form new memories for facts and events.

Helmet for my head
Protecting critical mass
Useful brain bucket.

RESEARCH has shown that wearing bicycle helmets
can reduce the risk of head injury up to 85%.

MRI, PET scan
New technology for all
Peer inside the brain.

RECENT TECHNOLOGY has enabled scientists to see inside the living brain. These brain imaging methods help us understand the relationships between specific areas of the brain and what function they serve, locate the areas of the brain that are affected by neurological disorders, and develop new strategies to treat brain disorders. MRI (magnetic resonance imaging) involves the detection of radio frequency signals produced by displaced radio waves in a magnetic field. It provides an anatomical view of the brain. PET (positron-emission tomography) scans detect radioactive material that is injected or inhaled to produce an image of the brain. This method provides a functional view of the brain.

Working all day long
Busy dog neurologist
Performing PET scans.

PET SCANS, which provide a functional image of the
brain, are used to study brain blood flow and diag-
nose neurological disorders.

Only 10 percent
Most sitting unused, fallow
It cannot be true.

IT IS A MYTH that we use only 10% of our brain. Clinical and experimental data show that we use all of our brain.

Electrical storm
Crossing corpus callosum
Epileptic curse.

THE WORD *epilepsy* comes from a Greek word meaning "to possess, seize, or hold." Because the brain uses electrochemical energy, any disruption of the electrical processes in the brain may cause abnormal functioning. Unfortunately, this is what happens during epilepsy: Neurons in the cerebral hemispheres misfire and create abnormal electrical activity like an electrical brainstorm. The seizure prevents the brain from interpreting and processing incoming sensory signals and from controlling muscles. The electrical storm can cross from one cerebral hemisphere through the corpus callosum, a collection of nerve fibers that connects the right and left hemispheres.

Weak invertebrate
The spineless, frail jellyfish
No backbone, no brain.

INVERTEBRATES, such as jellyfish, are animals without backbones (spinal column) or spinal cords. These animals are useful to study because their nervous systems function in a way similar to that of vertebrates. Because the nervous systems of invertebrates are less complex than those of vertebrates, it is easier to isolate and study neural functions in these animals.

Sodium is first
Entering open channels
Potassium next.

ACTION POTENTIALS are caused by an exchange of
ions across the neuron membrane. A stimulus first
causes sodium channels to open. Because there are
many more sodium ions on the outside of a neuronal
membrane and the inside of the neuron is negative
relative to the outside, sodium ions rush into the
neuron. Sodium has a positive charge, so the neuron
becomes more positive and becomes depolarized. It
takes longer for potassium channels to open. When
potassium channels do open, potassium rushes
out of the cell, reversing the depolarization. Also,
at about this time, sodium channels start to close.
This causes the action potential to go back toward

–70 millivolts (a repolarization). The action potential actually goes past –70 millivolts (a hyperpolarization) because the potassium channels stay open a bit too long. Gradually, the ion concentrations go back to resting levels and the cell returns to –70 millivolts.

Node of Ranvier
Gaps between myelin segments
Speeds spike conduction.

INFORMATION TRAVELS faster in axons that are insulated with myelin. Myelin is produced by glial support cells. Myelin wraps around the axon and helps electrical current flow down the axon (just like wrapping tape around a leaky water hose would help water flow down the hose). However, the myelin insulation does not cover the entire axon. Rather, there are breaks in the wrapping, called nodes of Ranvier. The distance between these nodes is between 0.2 and 2 millimeters. Action potentials traveling down the axon "jump" from node to node. This is called saltatory conduction, which means "to leap." Saltatory conduction increases the speed of an action potential traveling down an axon.

Ghostly, green flickers
Oscilloscope images
Streak past retinas.

AN OSCILLOSCOPE is an electronic device that
allows neuroscientists to see neuronal activity

Roof of mouth, skull base
Ate too fast, ice cream headache
Upsetting brain freeze.

ICE CREAM headaches ("brain freeze") occur when cold food is eaten too fast. These headaches are thought to be caused by rapid cooling of the palate, which then activates nerve fibers that cause pain. Rapid cooling may affect blood vessels, which change shape. This change in shape may activate nerve fibers that cause pain. The medical name for brain freeze is sphenopalatine ganglioneuralgia.

Fresh neurons arise
Call it neurogenesis
New tricks for old brains.

FOR MANY YEARS, it was believed that nerve cells in the adult brain, once damaged or dead, did not replace themselves. Recent data, however, have found that neurogenesis (the development of new neurons) is found in adults in several areas of the brain.

New neurons, old brains
Neurogenesis exists
In hippocampus.

THE HIPPOCAMPUS is one area of the brain where neurogenesis (the development of new neurons) occurs.

Sweet, gracious relief
Natural response to pain
Endorphin rescue.

IN RESPONSE to pain and stress, the brain produces chemicals called endorphins. Endorphins bind to opioid receptors to provide pain relief.

Wernicke damage
Meaningless word salad speech
Left-side injury.

PATIENTS with speech problems gave early research-
ers the first clues about how the brain is involved
with language. The loss of the ability to speak is
called aphasia. In 1876, Karl Wernicke found that
damage to the posterior part of the left temporal
lobe resulted in language problems such that speech
was incomprehensible.

Only word is "Tan"
Broca area lesion
Slow, disjointed speech.

IN 1861, Paul Broca described a patient who could say only one word: "Tan." Examination of Tan's brain revealed damage to part of the left frontal cortex, later known as Broca's area. People with Broca's aphasia have speech that is slow and difficult to understand.

Anger, happiness
Fear, sadness, joy, and despair
Limbic structures link.

THE LIMBIC SYSTEM (or the limbic areas) is a group
of connected structures that includes the amygdala,
the hippocampus, mammillary bodies, and the cingu-
late gyrus. These areas are important for controlling
the emotional response to a given situation and also
for memory.

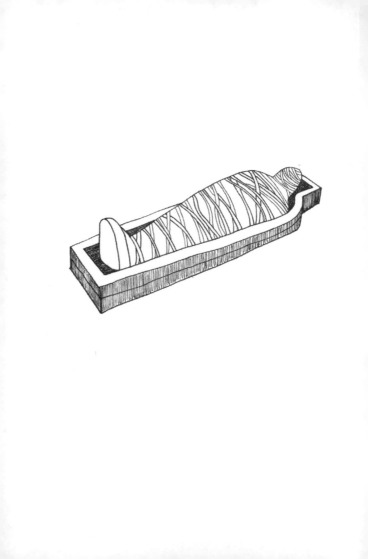

Egyptian mummy
Brain removed, discarded, scrap
Can it be the heart?

THE BRAIN was not always held in high regard. The ancient Egyptians, when creating a mummy, scooped out the brain through the nostrils and threw it away, believing it to be without value. The heart and other internal organs were removed carefully and preserved. These organs were then placed back in the body or in jars that were set next to the body.

Without impulses
Glia are forgotten cells
Appearance deceives.

ALTHOUGH GLIAL CELLS do not conduct action
potentials like neurons, they are essential for proper
functioning of the brain. Glia provide physical and
nutritional support for neurons, clean up brain
debris, transport nutrients to neurons, digest parts
of dead neurons, regulate the content of extracel-
lular space, and provide insulation to neurons to
increase conduction velocity.

Sliced, diced in small box
Locating genius complex
Albert Einstein's brain.

ALBERT EINSTEIN'S brain has been the subject of several studies investigating the neural basis of genius. These studies suggest that Einstein's brain shows differences in neuronal density, ratio of glia to neurons, and pattern of sulci. The interpretation of these data is controversial because similar studies in other highly intelligent people have not yet been performed.

Tongue taste sensations
Bitter, sour, salty, sweet
Now add umami.

THE TONGUE has taste buds that contain specialized receptor cells for chemicals. There are five basic tastes: bitter, sour, salty, sweet, and umami. Umami is a flavor that is tasted when foods with glutamate (like MSG) are eaten.

**EEG awake
Muscles paralyzed, eyes move
Paradoxical.**

DREAMING OCCURS most often during a stage of sleep called rapid eye movement (REM) sleep. During REM periods, brain wave patterns are similar to those when a person is awake. However, voluntary muscles are completely paralyzed and people cannot move. For this reason, REM sleep is sometimes referred to as paradoxical sleep.

Factory of dreams
Electrochemical stew
Never-ending buzz.

THE BRAIN is always active. Using electrochemical signals, neurons send messages throughout the body. Even during sleep, the brain is working.

Suddenly severe
Blocking, bleeding, brain attack
Weak, dizzy, silent.

A STROKE, also called a brain attack, occurs when the blood supply to the brain is stopped. If this condition lasts long enough, neurons will start to die because they will not get enough oxygen. A stroke can cause a variety of symptoms including dizziness and movement problems.

Depressing, sad thoughts
Overwhelming daily life
Purple haze surrounds.

DEPRESSION is a common mental illness in which people lose interest in activities, have trouble concentrating, withdraw from society, and have reduced energy levels.

Taste shapes, smell numbers
Synesthesia episode
Sensory mixing.

SYNESTHESIA is a condition in which one sense is simultaneously perceived as if by one or more additional senses. One form of synesthesia joins objects such as letters, shapes, numbers, or people's names with a sensory perception such as smell, color, or flavor. The word *synesthesia* comes from two Greek words, *syn* (together) and *aisthesis* (perception). Therefore, synesthesia literally means "joined perception."

Little batteries
Electricity blossoms
Neurons operate.

NEURONS are like little batteries because they generate a little bit of electricity.

Brain plaques and tangles
Memory loss, dementia
You are someone else.

BRAIN PLAQUES and tangles are characteristic features of the brains of patients with Alzheimer's disease. Tangles and plaques interfere with neuronal functions and may be responsible for memory loss and dementia.

We think we think thoughts
Speeding through slender pathways
Connections spring forth.

NEURAL SIGNALS are sent from the neuron cell body
down thin fibers called axons. Connections between
neurons create neuronal circuits that are responsible for thought and behavior.

Eight bone protector
Dura, arachnoid, pia
Guardians of thought.

THE BRAIN is surrounded by eight bones: one frontal bone, two parietal bones, two temporal bones, one occipital bone, one sphenoid bone, and one ethmoid bone. These eight bones make up the cranium. Another 14 bones in the face make up the entire skull. Below the skull are three special coverings called the meninges. The outer layer of the meninges is called the dura mater or just the dura. The dura is tough and thick, and it can restrict the movement of the brain within the skull. This protects the brain from movements that may stretch and break brain blood vessels. The middle layer of the meninges is called the arachnoid. The inner layer, the one closest to the brain, is called the pia mater or just the pia.

Clear, cloudless fluid
Circulate through ventricles
Protect, excrete, buoy.

THE ENTIRE SURFACE of the central nervous system
is bathed in a clear, colorless fluid called cerebro-
spinal fluid (CSF). The CSF is contained within a
system of fluid-filled cavities called ventricles. CSF
is produced mainly by a structure called the cho-
roid plexus in the lateral, third, and fourth ventricles. The CSF protects the brain from damage by
buffering the brain. In other words, the CSF acts to
cushion a blow to the head and lessen the impact.
It also reduces pressure at the base of the brain by
helping the brain float. The CSF also helps with the
excretion of waste products of the brain and serves
to transport hormones to other areas of the brain.

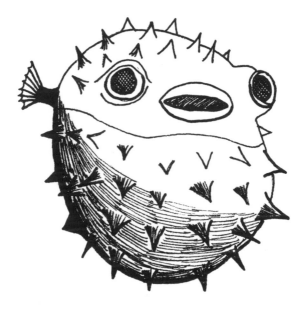

Tetrodotoxin
Deadly, toxic puffer fish
Careful with fugu!

TETRODOTOXIN is a neurotoxin found in the puffer fish. This neurotoxin works by blocking sodium channels on neurons, thereby preventing the generation of an action potential. Puffer fish is eaten as a delicacy called fugu.

Intense joy, delight
Serotonin depletion
Rave on Ecstasy.

THE DRUG Ecstasy is a central nervous system stimulant. Although the drug may induce pleasurable sensations, it has been shown to damage neurons that use the neurotransmitter called serotonin.

Developing brain
Adding neurons, synapses
To be pruned later.

DURING DEVELOPMENT, the brain produces many
neurons and connections that are lost or "pruned"
later in life.

Tremor, slow movement
Dopamine is diminished
Parkinson's disease.

PARKINSON'S DISEASE is a neurodegenerative disorder characterized by tremor (shaking), slowness of movement and rigidity, and loss of the neurotransmitter called dopamine. Parkinson's disease afflicts approximately 1 million to 1.5 million people in the United States, most of whom are at least 60 years old. The disorder is seen in people of all ethnic groups and among men and women in equal numbers. There is no known cause and no cure, just treatments to help control the symptoms. Parkinson's disease occurs when neurons degenerate (lose the ability to function normally) in a part of the brain called the substantia nigra. Many of these neurons that degenerate contain the neurotransmitter called dopamine. As these neurons degenerate, dopamine levels fall, and the balance between dopamine and other neurotransmitters, such as acetylcholine, is thrown off. This neurotransmitter imbalance affects the way muscles work and leads to movement problems.

Muhammad Ali
Michael J. Fox, Pope John Paul
Lacking dopamine.

MUHAMMAD ALI, Michael J. Fox, and Pope John Paul II are or were affected by Parkinson's disease, a neurodegenerative disorder that destroys neurons that contain the neurotransmitter called dopamine.

Challenged with puzzles
Mentally stimulated
Aged brain survives.

MENTAL STIMULATION, such as doing crossword puzzles, may be one way to reduce the risk of age-related neurological disorders such as Alzheimer's disease.

Selective membrane.
Negative, positive charge
It has potential.

WHEN A NEURON is not sending a signal, it is said to be at rest. When a neuron is at rest, the inside of the neuron is negative relative to the outside. Although the concentrations of the different ions attempt to balance on both sides of the membrane, they cannot because the cell membrane allows only some ions to pass through channels (ion channels). At rest, potassium ions can cross through the membrane easily. Also at rest, chloride ions and sodium ions have a more difficult time crossing. The negatively charged protein molecules inside the neuron cannot cross the membrane. In addition to these selective ion channels, there is a pump that uses energy to move three sodium ions out of the neuron for every two potassium ions it puts in. Finally, when all these forces balance, and the difference in the voltage between the inside and outside of the neuron is measured, you have the resting potential. The resting membrane potential of a neuron is about -70 millivolts—this means that the inside of the neuron is 70 millivolts less than the outside. At rest, there are relatively more sodium ions outside the neuron and more potassium ions inside that neuron.

Flintstone's chemical
Inhibitory signal
GABA-dabba-doo!

NEURONS COMMUNICATE with each other using chemicals called neurotransmitters. One major neurotransmitter that reduces the likelihood that an action potential will be generated in the next neuron is called GABA (gamma-aminobutyric acid).

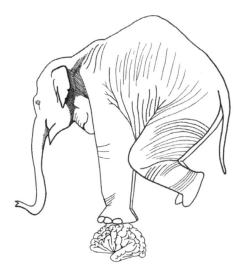

Elephant on brain
"You have a lot on your mind"
Neurologist says.

A NEUROLOGIST is a medical doctor who diagnoses
and treats disorders of the nervous system.

Between both your eyes
Olfactory sensations
Something for smelling.

OLFACTION IS the sense of smell.

Not your average
Butcher's salami slicer
Microtome sections.

A MICROTOME is a device that uses a sharp blade to cut the brain into thin slices. The slices can be stained to visualize neurons or glial cells and placed on slides for examination under a microscope.

Action potential
Negative to positive
Sending messages.

AN ACTION POTENTIAL is a sequential change in electrical membrane potential of a neuron. Action potentials occur when a neuron sends information down an axon, away from the cell body. This signal is an explosion of electrical activity that is created when some event (a stimulus) causes sodium channels to open. This causes the resting potential to become more positive and may result in the firing of an action potential. A short time later, potassium channels will open and potassium will leave the neuron. This will cause the membrane potential to become more negative.

Little sugar pill
Reduce my pain, placebo
I must please doctors.

A PLACEBO is a drug or treatment that has no active ingredient. For example, patients may receive a sugar pill instead of a real drug. It is important to have some subjects in every experiment receive the placebo treatment to separate the real effects of a drug or treatment from the effects of merely being in the experiment. The word *placebo* comes from the Latin phrase meaning "I will please."

Neurotransmitters
Lock-and-key mechanism
Membrane receptors.

NEUROTRANSMITTERS ARE chemicals that relay signals from neuron to neuron. The structure of a neurotransmitter is such that it fits into an appropriate receptor on a neuron like a key fits into a lock.

Its size is the same
It's either go or no go
It's all or nothing.

WHEN AN ACTION potential travels down the length
of an axon, it is always the same size and, once
started, it will travel the entire extent of the neuron.
This process is named the all-or-nothing principle of
neurotransmission.

Never-ending work
Thinking, planning, and learning
Even when asleep.

THE BRAIN works even when people are asleep. Experiments have demonstrated that sleep is important to consolidate memories.

Blind spots are present
Unless you're an octopus
Who doesn't have one.

THE BLIND SPOT is an area on the retina without receptors that respond to light. This region corresponds to the location where the optic nerve exits the eye on its way to the brain. The octopus does not have a blind spot because photoreceptors in the octopus retina are located in the inner portion of the eye and the cells that carry information to the brain are located in the outer portion of the retina. Therefore, in the octopus, photoreceptors are the first layer of the retina to be struck by light. In contrast, in humans, light must pass through several retinal layers before it stimulates photoreceptors.

I get along fine

Without a nervous system

We sponges march on.

THE SPONGE is the only multicellular animal without
a nervous system.

A butterfly tastes
Using willowy thin feet
Careful where they step.

A BUTTERFLY has taste receptors on its feet.

Internal cycles
Come circadian rhythms
All in a day's work.

CIRCADIAN RHYTHMS, internal body cycles that vary throughout the day, are regulated by the brain. Examples of circadian rhythms include the sleep cycle, alertness, body temperature, hormone levels, blood pressure, reaction time, hunger, and thirst.

Amphetamine high
Stimulate nervous system
Corrupt synapses.

AMPHETAMINES are drugs that stimulate the central nervous system and sympathetic division of the peripheral nervous system. The main action of amphetamines is to increase the synaptic activity of the dopamine and norepinephrine neurotransmitter systems. Amphetamines can cause the release of dopamine from axon terminals, block dopamine reuptake, inhibit the storage of dopamine in vesicles, and inhibit the destruction of dopamine by enzymes.

Dopamine, GABA
Serotonin, glutamate
Elixirs for brains.

NEURONS communicate with each other using chemicals called neurotransmitters. Major neurotransmitters include dopamine, GABA, serotonin, and glutamate.

I have amnesia
Anterograde, retrograde
Sometimes I forget.

AMNESIA is partial or complete loss of memory.
Anterograde amnesia is the inability to hold new
memories; retrograde amnesia is the loss of old
memories.

Twelve pairs of thin nerves
Sensory, motor, or both
The cranial nerves.

THE CRANIAL NERVES are 12 pairs of nerves that can be seen on the ventral (bottom) surface of the brain. Some of these nerves bring information from sense organs to the brain, control muscles, or are connected to glands or internal organs such as the heart and lungs.

It is a mouthful
Glossopharyngeal nerve
Cranial nerve nine.

THE GLOSSOPHARYNGEAL NERVE is the ninth cranial nerve. This nerve is responsible for taste from the back third of the tongue and touch information from the tongue, tonsils, and pharynx. It also controls some muscles used in swallowing.

Vibration sensors
High-frequency following
Pacinian cells.

THE SKIN has a variety of specialized receptors that respond to different types of stimulation. Pacinian corpuscles are one type of sensory receptor in the skin; they respond to high-frequency vibration.

A-delta fibers
Small-diameter axons
Thin myelin coating.

INFORMATION about touch and pain is transmitted to the spinal cord and brain by primary afferent axons. These are the nerve fibers connected to the different types of receptors in the skin, muscle, and internal organs. These primary afferent axons come in different diameters and can be divided into different groups based on their size. A-delta nerve fibers have a small diameter and are insulated with myelin.

Must move, must move now
Strange sensory sensation
Restless legs syndrome.

RESTLESS LEGS SYNDROME (RLS) is a disorder characterized by an urge to move in order to stop unpleasant sensory sensations, usually affecting the legs. This common neurological disorder affects 5–15% of the population in the United States. People with RLS experience these unpleasant feelings when they are at rest or lying down, ready to sleep. Therefore, people with RLS may have trouble falling asleep and staying asleep. This can lead to insomnia and sleepiness during the day and then to other problems such as depression and anxiety.

Brains are quite polite
Say hello to each other
With friendly brain waves.

BRAIN WAVES are the patterns of electrical activity generated by neurons and recorded using an electroencephalograph. Different brain waves (alpha, beta, delta, theta) are named for when they were discovered, not their frequencies.

An "X" marks the spot
On ventral side of the brain
Optic chiasm.

INFORMATION from the right and left visual fields crosses to the other side of the brain. This occurs in the optic chiasm, where the optic tracks cross. After the optic chiasm, information about the right visual field travels to the left side of the brain, and information about the left visual field travels to the right side. The word *chiasm* comes from Greek meaning "crossing."

Eye can see you now
Using both my optic nerves
Visual fields cross.

THE OPTIC NERVE is the second cranial nerve. The use of two eyes provides animals with binocular vision and enables a wider visual field and depth perception.

Right, left hemispheres
Separate down the middle
Perhaps seizures gone.

SEPARATING the right and left hemispheres by cutting the corpus callosum may reduce seizures in people with epilepsy. This surgery, called a corpus callosotomy or split brain operation, may be done when other treatments fail to control seizures. This procedure is done to prevent the spread of the seizure from one side of the brain to the other but can eliminate seizures completely.

Horizontal cut
Coronal, sagittal too
The planes of section.

SPECIAL WORDS are used to describe the position and direction of brain structures. These words help describe the location of structures relative to other structures. The brain, like all biological structures, is three dimensional. So, any point on or inside the brain can be localized on three axes or planes. The brain is often cut (sectioned) into pieces for further study. These slices are usually made in one of three planes: the coronal plane, the horizontal plane, or the sagittal plane.

Use a neural net
In the absence of a brain
To catch jellyfish.

A JELLYFISH has a nervous system of interconnected nerve cells (a neural net), but no brain. The nerve net conducts impulses around the entire body of the jellyfish. The strength of a behavioral response is proportional to the stimulus strength. In other words, the stronger the stimulus, the larger the response.

Tyrannosaurus
A very large stressed reptile
You're a nervous rex.

THE *TYRANNOSAURUS rex* was a large, carnivorous
dinosaur.

Memorize and learn
Reorganize synapses
It's plasticity.

PLASTICITY, or neuroplasticity, is the lifelong ability of the brain to reorganize neural pathways based on new experiences. As we learn, we acquire new knowledge and skills through instruction or experience. In order to learn or memorize a fact or skill, there must be persistent functional changes in the brain that represent the new knowledge. This ability of the brain to change with learning is what is known as neuroplasticity.

Neglect, depression
Mood swings, nausea, habit
Tolls of addiction.

DRUGS of abuse may give rise to many signs and symptoms that result in problems with friends, family, and coworkers.

Strange homunculus
Little man inside the brain
My, what large fingers.

AREAS OF SKIN with a higher density of somatosensory receptors (such as the face, hands, and fingers) have more cortical tissue devoted to them. If a body were built in proportion to the amount of cortex devoted to each part, it would look distorted, with a big head and hands, a small torso, and tiny legs. This distorted body map is called a homunculus, which means "little man."

PEOPLE

Acetylcholine
Fluid neurotransmitter
Wake Otto Loewi.

AUSTRIAN SCIENTIST Otto Loewi dreamed of the experiment to demonstrate that nerve cells release a chemical neurotransmitter (acetylcholine). On the night of Easter in 1921, Loewi woke up, wrote down his dream, and then went back to sleep. When he woke up the next morning, he could not read what he had written. The next night, he went to sleep, woke up at 3 a.m., and remembered the dream he had the previous night. This time, he went straight to the laboratory and performed an experiment to show that neurons use chemical signals.

Defining neurons
Connected or separate
Cajal, Golgi feud.

SPANIARD Santiago Ramón y Cajal and Italian Camillo Golgi shared the 1906 Nobel Prize in Physiology or Medicine. However, they disagreed about how nerve cells were connected to each other.

Sir Charles Sherrington
A synapse to join neurons
To clasp together.

IN 1897, Charles Sherrington coined the term *synapse* to describe the functional connection between neurons. The word *synapse* comes from the Greek *syn* meaning "together," and *haptein* meaning "to clasp."

Visual cortex
Bars of light, columns of cells
Hubel and Wiesel.

DAVID HUBEL and Torsten Wiesel won the 1981 Nobel Prize in Physiology or Medicine for their work on the processing of information in the visual system.

Infectious prions
Mad cow disease vehicle
Stanley Prusiner.

STANLEY PRUSINER won the 1997 Nobel Prize in Physiology or Medicine for the discovery of prions, a form of infection that is thought to underlie mad cow disease and other neurological diseases.

Research scientist
Manuscript preparations
Publish or perish.

RESEARCH SCIENTISTS must publish their work in journals to be promoted to higher-level positions.

Map cortex surface
Stimulate brain, remove harm
Neurosurgeons work.

NEUROSURGEONS electrically stimulate the brain to determine what tissue can be removed without affecting important functions.

Aristotle writes
Mental processes in heart
Plato is correct.

THE PHILOSOPHER Aristotle believed that the heart was responsible for mental processes. He wrote, "The seat of the soul and the control of voluntary movement—in fact, of nervous functions in general,—are to be sought in the heart. The brain is an organ of minor importance." Plato believed that the brain was responsible for these functions.

Tremors in aged
Essay on shaking palsy
Writes James Parkinson.

IN 1817, James Parkinson published a manuscript titled "An Essay on the Shaking Palsy" to describe tremor (shaking) and other symptoms of a disorder that now bears his name (Parkinson's disease).

Large, small nerve fibers
Melzack, Wall control theory
Closed gate, reduced pain.

IN 1965, Patrick Wall and Ronald Melzack published their work on the gate control theory. This theory explains how pain is a function of the balance between the information traveling into the spinal cord through large and small nerve fibers.

Poor Phineas Gage
Iron rod pierces his brain
Still famous today.

IN 1848, railroad worker Phineas Gage suffered an accident when a 3 foot tamping rod pierced his skull and frontal lobe. Although Mr. Gage survived the accident, damage to his frontal lobe changed his personality from calm and capable to crass and impatient.

Eric Kandel works
Memory mechanisms
Hand me a sea hare.

ERIC KANDEL won the 2000 Nobel Prize in Physiology or Medicine for his work on learning and memory. His studies focused primarily on the nervous system of the *Aplysia* (sea hare).

Aquatic doctor
Submarine brain surgery
A neurosturgeon?

A NEUROSURGEON is a medical doctor who performs surgery on the nervous system; a sturgeon is a type of fish.

Skull bumps can reveal
Intellect and emotions
According to Gall.

FRANZ JOSEPH GALL developed the theory of phrenology, proposing that intellectual and personality traits could be read by the bumps on the skull. Although phrenology was popular in the 19th century, there is no scientific evidence to support the practice.

Make lesions Lashley
Brain mass, not the location
All is not equal.

KARL LASHLEY believed that total brain area, not specific brain locations, was responsible for cognitive abilities.

Hodgkin and Huxley
Transmission of impulses
Squid giant axon.

ALAN LLOYD HODGKIN and Andrew Fielding Huxley won the 1963 Nobel Prize in Physiology or Medicine for their work describing how neurons send signals. They performed critical experiments using the giant axon of a squid.

Dual consciousness
Sperry split right from the left
Two brains per person?

ROGER SPERRY won the 1981 Nobel Prize in Physiology or Medicine for his work showing that the right and left sides of the brain are specialized for different tasks.

Medical marvel
Cures for spinal cord damage
Thank you, Christopher.

ACTOR CHRISTOPHER REEVE suffered a severe spinal cord injury in 1995 when he was thrown from a horse. He established a foundation that supports research to treat and cure paralysis caused by spinal cord injury. Reeve passed away in 2004.

Stained shirts, pants, bibs, socks
Neuroanatomist's child
Cresyl violet next.

CRESYL VIOLET is a common stain used by neuro-
anatomists to visualize the cell bodies of neurons.